1,00

C0-ASM-831

MOTHER'S

MEDITATIONS

Marie Frost

 Heritage Edition

MOTHER'S MEDITATIONS

Library of Congress Card Catalog No. 68-56397

Copyright © 1968 by Tyndale House Publishers
Wheaton, Illinois

Printed in U.S.A.

No Regrets

Keep your eyes on Jesus."—Hebrews 12:2

"Mommy!" Ellie screamed, running into the room. "Junior kicked me!"

"I did not!"

"You did! You did! You did!"

Mother sighed: The minute she had a chance to sit down and type this important letter . . . if only she could send the children outside to play!

But a wistful glance at the window showed the weather had no intention of favoring her wish. "I'll tell you what," Mother said brightly as she comforted three teary-eyed little ones, "let's play a game. Let's pretend that this is the very last day we will ever have before Jesus comes. That means that today we'll want to be kind and do all the things that would please Him."

Rather pleased with herself, Mother hurried the children back into the playroom, firmly shut the door, and sat down to type again.

But immediately there was pandemonium in the playroom and soon the door flew open. "Oh, Mommy!" Ellie wailed this time. "Junior still treats me as if I were going to be here *all my life!*"

Are you treating your family as if they were always going to be around? They aren't, you know. Little ones grow up and leave. Heart attacks snatch away adults. Brothers and sisters move away and become like strangers. Parents quietly pass on, long before we're ready for them to.

Regret is a sad and futile thing. Determine now to live today and every day so that tomorrow there will be no regrets.

BIBLE READING: Titus 2

TODAY I WILL PRAY FOR:

_____

Like a Father

He is like a father to us, tender and sympathetic to those who reverence Him. For He knows we are but dust.—Psalm 103: 13, 14

The last child had been tucked in after the final "one-more-drink," and the house was quiet. Time at last, Mother thought gratefully, to clean up after the long day and get ready for tomorrow.

But after an hour of sweeping, picking up, and putting away, I heard a muffled but unmistakable sound. Jay was coughing again.

Taking the stairs two at a time, I remembered frantically the many long, sleepless nights I had spent with little Jay shaking in my arms with asthmatic attacks. How often he had seemed ready to slip away, only to be restored by a merciful God!

But, now as I opened his door, in the old creaky rocker sat my husband, tenderly holding the frail little body of his son against his own strong, warm one, and comforting him with the manly love only a father can show . . . the same love our heavenly Father showers—tender and sympathetic—on each of His dear children.

"Wrap yourself" in that love. Its warmth and strength can carry you with joy through the most difficult times.

BIBLE READING: Psalm 103

TODAY I WILL PRAY FOR:

_____

Time to Listen

O God, you have helped me from my earliest childhood—and I have constantly testified to others of the wonderful things you do.— Psalm 71:17

The responsibilities of day-in, night-out care of babies, children, or teen-agers demand adult strength, adult wisdom, and adult acceptance. How wistfully we sometimes look at our teen-agers or at other young people around us, envying their days of carefree pleasure!

But think back to your teen-age days; were *they* really carefree? Or were they full of innumerable crises: the dress that didn't fit; the words that came out all wrong; the heartbreaking crushes of puppy love; the coat that was always, irrevocably, the wrong color; the hair that wouldn't keep its curl; the nose that was too big and unbeautiful; the figure that was too fat or too thin or too tall or too short; parental quarrels; doubts about God and moral laws, the panicky feeling deep inside that no one really loved you or cared?

Clothes and other fads change, but teen-agers are the same inside in all generations. How long has it been since you—instead of letting your sharp words fly—took time to *listen* to your teen-ager? Or how long since you tried to be friends with and pray for the teen-agers in your block, at your church?

The decisions they make now can change their lives. Are you a caring Christian?

BIBLE READING: I Corinthians 13

TODAY I WILL PRAY FOR:

Drastically Marked
Down

These will be His royal titles: "Wonderful,"
"Counselor," "The Mighty God," "The Ever-
lasting Father," "The Prince of Peace." —
Isaiah 9: 6

Hardly are the Christmas decorations down
before the "January Sale" signs are up. The
things for which there was such a great demand a week ago are now superfluous and
taking up space needed for the next season's
merchandise.

"Now Drastically Marked Down" are
Christmas trees, ornamental angels, Christmas
cards and tree ornaments, even items in the

Religious Goods department. One such store advertised, "All Bibles Marked Down," "50% Off" on pictures of Christ and on crucifixes.

Now that Christmas is over, has the Bible been "marked down" at your house: Do its precious stories and truths seem less important now that Christmas vacation is over and the family is busy once more doing the "important" things of life? Do childish eyes that sparkled at the Christmas angel on your tree still glow wonderingly each night as you read to them from your Bible or Bible-story book? Or do you skip the Bible reading now and substitute a quick kiss?

Is Christ now "50% Off" in your home? Christ must not only be Lord of Christmas, but of every single day.

BIBLE READING: Hebrews 1

TODAY I WILL PRAY FOR:

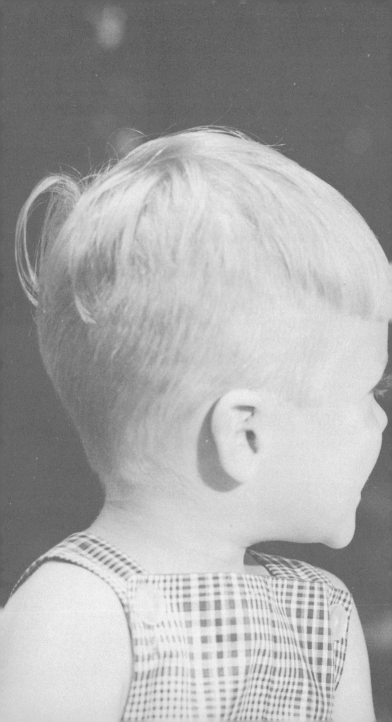

No Time

Her sister Mary sat spellbound on the floor,
listening to Jesus as He talked.—Luke 10: 39

There's dinner to fix and batter to mix
And a hundred and one things to do—
Clothes to be laundered and hung up and
dried,
And dusting and vacuuming, too!
So busy this life, so hurried and quick,
No time to be still; no stop—all go!
No time to pray to the Lord today!

"No time, My child, to be still and
know?"
But there's sweeping and sewing and
scrubbing and shining
And clothes to be mended and folded and
hung
And drawers to be tidied and notes to be
answered
And shoppers and shelves to go shopping
among.

No time to stop and get down on my knees!
Prayer and my Bible? I've no time for these—
I've my family to keep!
I'll pray, though, tonight—if I don't fall
   asleep.

   "My child, My child, I can only weep.

   You are cumbered with much; don't you
know that I care?

   How gladly all of your trials I'd share!

   Just sit at My feet and taste of My
Word—

   When last, My child, have you read it,
or heard?

   Martha the service of Mary did ask,

   But Mary took MY strength to help in
her task.

   That strength, My child, is waiting
and free.

   Try it now—and see!"

BIBLE READING: Luke 10:38-42

TODAY I WILL PRAY FOR:

_____

Ears That Hear Not

I am listening to all the Lord is saying.—
Psalm 85:8

"Mommy," remarked five-year-old Penny, "I know now what I'm going to be when I grow up."

"You do, dear? What?"

"A nurse. God told me."

"Aw, God wouldn't tell you a thing like that," scoffed older brother George.

"Yes, He did," Penny replied serenely. "He just talked and I listened."

Mother was nearby. "Did you ever talk to God about what you should be when you grow up, George?" she asked.

"Oh, of course not," George retorted. And then more soberly, " 'Sides, if I did, I just know He'd say, 'Be a preacher.' "

How many of us are like George—we don't listen to God because we're afraid we won't like what He has to say? We scurry to prayer, quickly say everything we think should be said, then scurry away before the Lord has a chance to begin His side of the conversation. We enter whole-heartedly into the singing at church, but close our ears when the message begins. We call Him "Father"—and yet don't even extend to Him the courtesy we expect of our own children!

It is not enough for a servant to say, "I will do whatever you tell me"—then run and hide so he cannot hear his master's words.

Has fear stuffed up your ears? Or a secret sin? Or plain old rebellion? Isn't it time to pull out those earplugs, and listen to the Word of God? God won't make you listen, but you'll never regret it if you do.

BIBLE READING: James 1:19-25

TODAY I WILL PRAY FOR:

Forgive and Forget

If you are angry, don't sin by nursing your grudge. Don't let the sun go down with you still angry—get over it quickly.—Ephesians 4:26

There has been a quarrel, and the air is still so heavy it would take a knife to cut it. You aren't speaking, but inwardly the words are seething, "It's all his fault ... he'll have to apologize first ... he just doesn't love me ... he doesn't care."

The tears spill and dry and spill some more.

His fault? Maybe ... but maybe it's your fault. Maybe both. Many a huff has been born through a simple misunderstanding. But this isn't the point.

"Then Peter came to Him and asked, 'Sir, how often should I forgive a brother who sins against me? Seven times?' 'No!' Jesus replied, 'seventy times seven'!" (Matthew 18:21, 22).

Love is a two-way street; bitterness can instantly stop all traffic on it. Say you're sorry about the fight, and open up the way to communication and forgiveness. Forgive and forget. Bury a dead problem.

Make "Let not the sun go down upon your wrath" a literal, daily rule in your house among both parents and children, that all may sleep in peace and love. Hard to do? Let God help you do it. He knows far more about love and forgiveness than we'll ever be able to learn!

BIBLE READING: Matthew 18:21-35

TODAY I WILL PRAY FOR:

_____

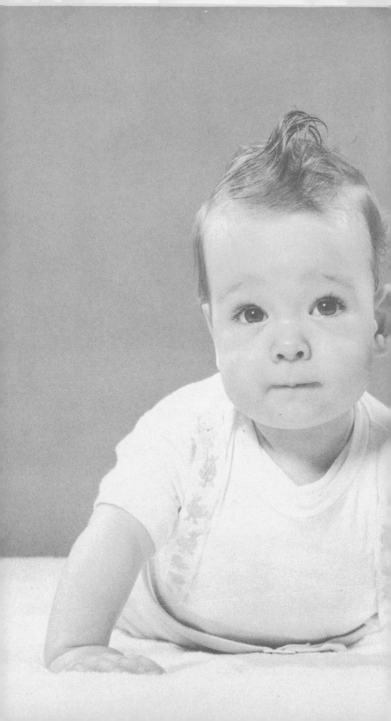

Rest Awhile

Let's get away for awhile and rest.—Mark 6:31

"Mother," one of my daughters said searchingly, "you know, all day long you've been thinking I've been doing things wrong. I don't think you're feeling good. Maybe you're getting a cold . . ."

What a start to think that maybe the trouble was not with my daughter, but with *me!* There are always more demands on a mother's time than she can take care of. Rooms must be cleaned, dresses need to be sewed, sick neighbors require help, homework can't wait until tomorrow. Even the moments that should be peaceful aren't. Somehow children are born with their volume turned all the way up—and manage to stay that way for the first 20 years or so!

Moments of peace, self-searching, and re-direction are necessary for maintaining a healthy state of mind and a stable household. But they won't be given you; you'll have to *take* them. John Wesley's mother found it best to get up in the quiet of the night when she could concentrate on the spiritual needs of her large family rather than on their physical ones. Perhaps for you the best time is the first 15 minutes or so after the last child leaves for school, in the afternoon when baby is having a nap, early in the morning before the rest of the family is up, or in the evening when the house is once more quiet.

Let's get away for awhile (and take time for Bible study and prayer) and rest.

BIBLE READING: Matthew 6:5-15

TODAY I WILL PRAY FOR:

_____

The Missing Ingredient

*You will keep on guiding me all my life with
your wisdom and counsel.*—Psalm 73:24

Auburn-haired Peggy wasn't the world's
brightest woman, but she had a heart of gold,
a lovely smile, and a determination to do everything she could for her children. The proof
was going to be a real birthday party for
five-year-old Timmy.

"Not just any cake will do for a birthday
party," Peggy decided, looking through her
cookbooks. And then she found it—the pièce
de résistance: The Cherry King Cream Supreme four-layer!

For days Peggy chatted about that cake.
The evening before the Big Day, she walked

to the store to buy all its ingredients from her thin purse, and the morning of the Big Day she baked it.

How eagerly the children rushed into the kitchen to see this masterpiece! But what a surprise. All four layers of the Cherry King Cream Supreme, icing included, were no thicker combined than the brave little candles topping it!

As the children solemnly tackled the soggy mess, Peggy admitted, "I guess I left something out."

What she had left out, she discovered, was the baking powder. "Oh, that," Peggy moaned; "I didn't think that was important."

Days of dreams and hours of work wasted, just because something had been left out. Most of us work and work at home, and at church too, wondering why our efforts fail "to rise" to our expectations, when our problem is that we're leaving Christ, His guidance, and His power out of it all. Ask Him—right now— to be with you in everything you do today that it may be done as He would have you do it.

BIBLE READING: Psalm 121

TODAY I WILL PRAY FOR:

Spiritual Closets

I am going to be a guest in your home today!—Luke 19:5b.

Mother's closet is usually the most-neglected one in the family. After all, Sis *has* to have something new for the Senior banquet; Dad *has* to have something to wear to work every day; Butch *has* to have pants long enough to cover his legs (even if he outgrows his pants before he outwears them). If someone can "make do," it can always be Mother.

And then comes that important, unexpected time when Mother must dress up. What a disappointment to open her closet door only to find she has "nothing to wear"; to try on her "best" dress only to discover it no longer fits, or has faded, or looks sadly out of date.

Our spiritual "clothes" can get out of date, too. Neglecting prayer, Bible reading, church attendance, and witnessing to our faith in Christ does not take away our salvation in Christ, but it does shrivel up our spiritual resources so that in times of real need we will find ourselves woefully inadequate.

Have you taken stock of your spiritual closet recently? Would you be prepared to welcome the Lord Jesus as your guest today?

BIBLE READING: Psalm 119:97-112

TODAY I WILL PRAY FOR:

_____

A Yard
Full of Diamonds

*Have you visited the treasuries of the snow
. . . ?*—Job 38:22a.

"Oh no, not another day of snow," I grumbled, peering out into the early morning darkness. And to make matters worse, the snow soon changed to sleet and ice. Driving was hazardous, schools were closed, the children were sick. Then the heavy storm felled power lines, cutting off all heat and power in 20°-below weather. What a miserable winter!

But eventually the clouds lifted a little, letting a wan sun come through. And then a little voice cried, "Oh, Mother! Come and see! Our yard is full of diamonds!"

Mother went to see, and the yard *was* full of diamonds ... the glittering of the sun on ice and snow. It was majestic, awesome, indescribably beautiful.

Only God could create such a white, still world. And the God who created it would care for it—and for us too.

Have *you* visited the treasuries of the snow?

BIBLE READING: Psalm 135:1-7

TODAY I WILL PRAY FOR:

———————————————————

A Cup of Water

If anyone so much as gives you a cup of water because you are Christ's—I say this solemnly —he won't lose his reward.—Mark 9:41

Elderly Mrs. Lemon had little of this world's goods, but an abundance of love and a warm sense of humor. Consequently, it was quite a treat for the children whenever she babysat with them.

"You know, you are very old," six-year-old Andy remarked one day, "but I like you anyway."

"Yes," replied Mrs. Lemon, a twinkle in her eyes; "almost one hundred years old, I guess."

"One hundred!" Andy repeated in astonishment. "Why, you're almost dead!" And he jumped up and ran out of the room.

When he finally came back, Mrs. Lemon wasn't sure what to expect. But Andy held out his little hands with a glowing smile. Inside was a crookedly folded piece of paper. "I want you to have this now while you can still see and smell," he explained.

Mrs. Lemon took the paper and opened it hesitantly. There was a hastily-drawn tulip of brightest red—it even smelled!

"Kay and me put some of Mother's perfume on it," Andy explained.

But even more attractive was something glittering high in the picture's "sky." "That's your crown for when you get to heaven," Andy said. "We put real sparkle on it for you."

For years afterward Mrs. Lemon cherished that picture. Such a little thing; just as small as "a cup of water." But little tokens of real love, however small, mean more to the sick, the lonely, the aged, than the most expensive bouquets . . . when it may be too late.

Are you giving lovingly to those around you "cups of water" in the name of Christ?

BIBLE READING: James 2:14-26

TODAY I WILL PRAY FOR:

_____

Oil for Troubled Waters

But the wisdom that comes from heaven is first of all pure and full of quiet gentleness. Then it is peace-loving and courteous. It allows discussion and is willing to yield to others, it is full of mercy and good deeds. It is wholehearted and straightforward and sincere.—James 3:17

Three-year-old Burt was suffering from "jealousitis." His baby brother had infringed upon his "rights" and Burt was ready to retaliate. He hadn't found any way to do so at home, however, but at nursery school he decided to be bolder.

"Now everybody listen to me," he announced to a half-dozen other pre-schoolers.

"I'm boss and I tell you what to do. Nobody can play with the blocks but me!"

Of course the other children completely ignored Burt's command, and immediately wholesale screaming and disorder broke out.

Such situations are expected among children ... but how sad when they happen among adults. "For wherever there is jealousy or selfish ambition" (no matter the position or age of the people involved), "there will be disorder and every other kind of evil"—James 3:15. "But the wisdom that is from *above* is first pure, then *peaceable....*"

Are your relationships and contacts with others full of peace—or of anger and discord? If you're the type who reacts to slight provocations or who takes all remarks personally and broods over them until you've built up a huge case of cold fury, there's only one place to "get even," or balanced again, and that is in the presence of God through faith in His Son, the Prince of Peace. Only He can clean your heart of those festering jealousies and grudges, and help you be fully at peace—both with others and with yourself.

BIBLE READING: Ephesians 4:22-32

TODAY I WILL PRAY FOR:

When the Way Is Rough

For when the way is rough, your patience has a chance to grow.—James 1:3

It had been a discouraging Sunday evening service. The weather was bleak, the crowd was unusually small, and it seemed that the pastor-husband's sermon wasn't "getting through"—at least not to me!

Why (I muttered to myself as he preached) should my husband have turned down offers from much larger churches to accept this mission effort—and now be preaching to a mere handful? It was obviously a waste of his time—and of God's!

The more I labored over this in my mind, the more convinced I became that we were simply not in God's place of appointment. After all, did not God bless those who were in

His will? And was not this pathetically poor attendance proof that He wasn't blessing us?

Just then I felt compelled to open God's Word and begin reading. My eye fell on these words:

"Dear brothers, is your life full of difficulties and temptations? Then be happy. For when the way is rough, your patience has a chance to grow"—James 1: 2, 3.

And suddenly all bitterness and discouragement left me. As better perspective returned, I began remembering all those who had recently come to know Christ as Savior through our Sunday school and our special weekday Bible classes. God *had* been blessing! And He would continue to bless as long as we gave out His Word in faith and obedience.

"Forgive me, God," I prayed. "And thank You for the congregation tonight, small as it is. You have used it to teach me not to try to squirm out of my problems, and to know the truth of Your Word: 'For when your patience is finally in full bloom, then you will be ready for anything, strong in character, full and complete'—James 1:4."

BIBLE READING: Romans 5:3-5

TODAY I WILL PRAY FOR:

With Eternity's Values in View

Don't store up your profits here on earth, where they erode away, and can be stolen! But store them in heaven, where they never lose their value, and are safe from thieves!—Matthew 6:19, 20

"Mike! Karen!" screamed Mrs. Kline above the howl of the approaching storm. "To the storm cellar—quick!"

"Mother!" Karen called as she saw her mother run toward the house. "Aren't you coming?"

"I'll be right there, Karen. I have to close some windows. Now—RUN!"

As the children dashed for safety, and Mrs. Kline dashed to close the upstairs windows, the sky was already turning frighteningly black. Suddenly—BOOM! Windows rattled, doors flew open, the whole house shook.

"Dear God, help!" cried Mrs. Kline. "A tornado!"

Hurling herself under a bed, she cringed at

the unearthly wind, the awesome sound of buildings and trees flying through the air.

"At least the children are safe ... and John at work. Oh, if only I had longer to live; things would be so different ... if only I'd taken time to pray with the children this morning ... gone to see Mike play ball last night as he begged me to ... gone to see that field of tulips John was aglow over ... listened to Kay's Bible verses ... spent more time with John, and really let him know I love him ... been more faithful in telling others about Christ. Oh, if only I had another chance!"

And then, as suddenly as it came, the storm passed. Mrs. Kline looked out at fantastic damage and heard the wail of sirens; but she and the children and John were all safe. God *had* given her another chance. . . .

"Dear God," she prayed with a heart overwhelmed with unworthiness and gratitude, "help me to realize my real treasures of a wonderful family and faith in Christ ... to learn to look at every day not just with everyday eyes, but with eternity's values in view."

BIBLE READING: Colossians 3:2

TODAY I WILL PRAY FOR:

_____

How Much Do We Trust God ?

Don't worry about anything; instead, pray about everything; tell God your needs and don't forget to thank Him for His answers. If you do this you will know God's peace which is far more wonderful than the human mind can understand. His peace will keep your thoughts and your hearts quiet and at rest as you trust in Christ Jesus.—Philippians 4:6,7

"Oh, Mother," Mark asked tearfully, "how can I remember to take my tennis shoes to school tomorrow? I've forgotten them for two days already!"

"Ask God to help you remember, dear," Mother suggested.

Later that evening as Mother was making her usual rounds to see that all were peacefully sleeping, she noticed in Mark's room two new tennis shoes, attached firmly to two little feet, sticking out from under a new white sheet.

"Why, Mark," she commented the next

morning, "why in the world did you wear your tennis shoes to bed last night?"

"Well, Mother," Mark explained, "I asked God to help me remember to wear them, like you told me to. And then I kept them on to help God help me remember!"

"Take your burdens to the Lord and leave them there," most of us sing glibly at church. But when the time really comes we are much more likely to take our burdens to the Lord—and then take them right back home.

How little we trust God! Do we really believe we are so much more able to handle our problems, frustrations, and heartaches than the One who made us—who is all-seeing, all-knowing, all-powerful, all-loving, all-wise?

We need to step out onto the waters of faith as Peter did, and at least *try* to walk its waves.

"O man of little faith," Jesus said, "why did you doubt?"—Matthew 14:31

"I *do* have faith; oh, help me to have more!"—Mark 9:23

BIBLE READING: Philippians 4:6,7; Matthew 14:31; Mark 9:24

TODAY I WILL PRAY FOR:

When Grandpa Sang

For it's not where we worship that counts, but how we worship—is our worship spiritual and real? Do we have the Holy Spirit's help?
For God is Spirit, and we must have His Spirit's help to worship as we should.—John 4: 22, 23

"We're playing church, Grandpa," cried out the children as their beloved grandfather—arriving on one of his rare visits—came into view. "Could you play with us, please?"

Grandpa's blue eyes twinkled under the graying brows as he walked over to the "church." In the wonderful way of children, the back porch had become a sanctuary; the porch railing, an organ; and a boot-box, the pulpit. Five-year-old Sue was an earnest organist. Seven-year-old Todd was a pastor, while little Kevin was glorying in his role as usher.

The sight warmed the heart of Grandpa—just as it warmed *my* heart—for I was peeking on the little scene from my kitchen window.

"Would you be the special music, Grandpa?" Todd asked.

And Grandpa, nodding solemnly, stood up, and in his old, cracked voice sang, "Great Is Thy Faithfulness."

The children listened quietly, and tears sprang to my eyes, because of the beauty of his singing ... not "beauty" as others might judge beauty, for his old voice no longer hinted any great quality it might once have possessed; but beauty springing from a life of love, trials, tribulations, and steadfastness, that had indeed determined that God's faithfulness was not only great, but infinite.

At that moment I would not have traded my privilege with the privilege of hearing the greatest, best-trained voice in the world ... especially if such voice, though able to sing stirringly about God, did not reflect a heart that truly loves the God about whom it sings, nor has known the joy of sins forgiven through God's dear Son.

For Grandpa, silver hair, cracking voice, and all, was indeed worshiping his heavenly Father "in spirit and in truth."

BIBLE READING: John 4:21-24

TODAY I WILL PRAY FOR:

The Crack in the Bat

Like an athlete I punish my body, treating it roughly, training it to do what it should, not what it wants to. Otherwise I fear that after enlisting others for the race, I myself might be declared unfit and ordered to stand aside.—I Corinthians 9:27

Proudly little Joe clutched the cracked bat that had been tossed aside by a college ball player.

"It's all yours," the coach had said. It didn't matter to Joe that the bat was cracked. After all, a little tape could fix that! What mattered was that he now had a genuine college baseball bat for his very own!

With great joy and gusto Joe carried his new possession home and carefully wrapped tape around it until the cracked part could no longer be seen. With great expectation and pride he carried it outside to play ball!

But, after trying the bat Joe returned to the house, choking with sobs and holding in each hand the bat's broken pieces. The tape that had made the bat look new had been unable to mend the crack on the inside. The crack, as the coach had known, had made the bat unfit for further use.

I know some once-wonderful Christians whose lives are like that bat. At one time their lives counted for God and they were "hitting a pretty good average" in using their talents for His glory. Others were blessed because of their works and glowing testimony.

Then, somehow, there came a "crack" and they were living for their Lord less and less. Ministers, laymen, missionaries—with vast reservoirs of unused abilities—laid aside and forgotten because they have left their "first love," their dedication and zeal for the One who saved them.

Are you in danger of becoming such a "castaway"? Remember that we leave God— God does not leave us. Confess any coldness right now, return fervently to the study of His Word, and He will fan the dying embers into a new flame of love and praise for Him and joy for yourself.

BIBLE READING: Psalm 31:12

TODAY I WILL PRAY FOR:

Resisting Temptation

And you can trust God to keep temptation from becoming so strong that you can't stand up against it.—I Corinthians 10:13

"Mommy," asked little Ann thoughtfully, "if God wants us to be good, how come He makes it so easy for us to be bad?"

How come indeed? We know that a plant grown indoors tends to be weak and spindly even with the best of care. It has not developed the strength necessary to withstand the scorching sun, beating rain, and biting wind. Just so, it takes the day-by-day accumulation of temptations met and mastered through the power of the Holy Spirit and the guidance of the Word to make the Christian strong, able to stand in times of great temptation and duress.

How are you growing?

BIBLE READING: Matthew 4:1-11

TODAY I WILL PRAY FOR:

_____

In Days of Sorrow

I have told you all this so that you will have peace of heart and mind. Here on earth you will have many trials and sorrows; but cheer up, for I have overcome the world.—John 16: 33

What a long winter it had been! Deep drifts of snow still blanketed the landscape. Would spring never come?

But, listen! Somewhere I hear a cardinal singing!

The children rush to the window to see this brave new friend—his bold red coat so easy to spot against the snow.

"Oh, Mother!" Sharon cries. "He's trying to tell us spring is almost here!"

"Spring always comes after winter," adds little Linda solemnly.

Ah, little ball of courage and feathers, I thought. You have seen the world today with your instincts, not your eyes. To us it is still winter, but you know that if winter is here, spring cannot be far behind. You walk by faith, not by sight, well attuned to the calendar of your heart.

Even as spring is the glory of the bird, so the day of being together with Christ for all eternity is the glory, the hope, the heartbeat of the Christian. No more death; no more pain; no more sorrow; no more suffering; no more shameful yielding to temptation.

Oh, that we might lift our eyes above that which is and keep before us that which is to be! What a marvelous cause for rejoicing!

"Be happy about it! Be very glad! for a tremendous reward awaits you up in heaven!"—Matthew 5:12.

"Then I, the King, shall say to those at My right, 'Come, blessed of My Father, into the Kingdom prepared for you from the founding of the world.' "—Matthew 25:34.

BIBLE READING: I Peter 1:7-13

TODAY I WILL PRAY FOR:

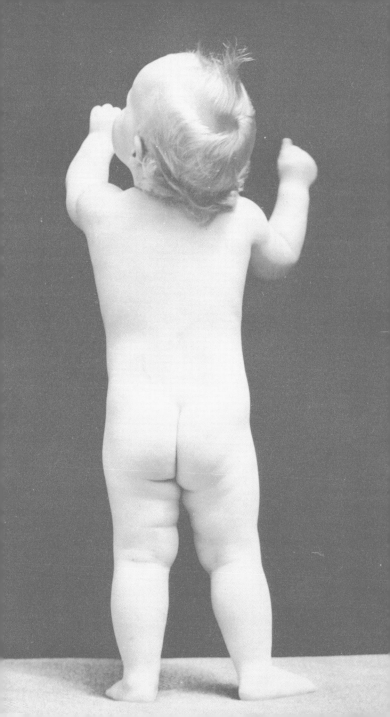